REDUCING WASTE

Anne Flounders

RED CHAIR
•PRESS•

Please visit our website at **www.redchairpress.com**.
Find a free catalog of all our high-quality products for young readers.

Reducing Waste

Publisher's Cataloging-In-Publication Data
(Prepared by The Donohue Group, Inc.)

Flounders, Anne.

Reducing waste / Anne Flounders.
p. : ill., maps ; cm. -- (Our green Earth)
Summary: Where does all the garbage go and why is it important to cut back on waste?
Discover why waste is creating problems for Earth and how you can help reduce, reuse, and
recycle now. Includes step-by-step ideas for taking action, different points of view, an up-close
look at relevant careers, and more.
Includes bibliographical references and index.
ISBN: 978-1-939656-46-9 (lib. binding/hardcover)
ISBN: 978-1-939656-34-6 (pbk.)
ISBN: 978-1-939656-53-7 (eBook)
1. Waste minimization--Juvenile literature. 2. Recycling (Waste, etc.)--Juvenile literature.
3. Environmental protection--Juvenile literature. 4. Waste minimization. 5. Recycling (Waste)
6. Environmental protection. I. Title.
TD792 .F56 2014

363.728   2013937165

Illustration credit: p. 8-9: Joe LeMonnier

Photo credits: Cover, title page, p. 4, 5, 8, 9, 15, 19, 21, back cover: Shutterstock; TOC, p. 12, 14,
16, 17, 18, 19, 20, 23, 24, 25, 26, 27, 31: Dreamstime; p. 7: Library of Congress; p. 10: Photographer,
Scuba Drew Wheeler, Courtesy of Algalita Marine Research Institute; p. 11: Paula S. Rose; p. 22:
Girl Scouts of the USA, all rights reserved; p. 25: Richard Hutchings; p. 28: AU Waste Reduction
& Recycling Dept.; p.32: © Hildi Todrin, Crane Song Photography

This series first published by:
Red Chair Press LLC   PO Box 333   South Egremont, MA 01258-0333

Printed in the United States of America

1 2 3 4 5 18 17 16 15 14

MIX
Paper from
responsible sources
FSC   FSC® C002589
www.fsc.org

TABLE OF CONTENTS

CHAPTER ONE
What is Waste?....................................4

CHAPTER TWO
Reduce, Reduce, Reduce 12

CHAPTER THREE
Reuse and Recycle................................ 20

ON THE JOB: DONNY ADDISON 28

GLOSSARY...30

FOR MORE INFORMATION 31

INDEX 32

What is Waste?

Lunch time! Here's a sandwich wrapped in foil. A plastic cup of yogurt and a plastic spoon. Milk in a carton. A granola bar in a wrapper. An orange. After lunch, the foil, cup, spoon, carton, wrapper, and orange peels go into the garbage. Lunch is over in about 20 minutes. But the story of the garbage is just beginning.

What is Waste?

Waste is another word for garbage. If we do not need something, and we throw it away, that is waste. People have always created waste. Throughout history, people have dealt with the problem of what to do with it. People mostly buried their garbage or burned it. In U.S. cities in the 1800s, people put their waste in the streets. Pigs were put to work eating the garbage. But of course, pigs create waste of their own. Horses also added to that mess. And if an animal died, it often just stayed where it was. City streets tended to smell pretty bad during that time!

All that waste out in the open made people sick. In 1866, New York City's board of health had to pass a law forbidding people from dumping garbage, ashes, or dead animals in the streets. The turn of the 20th century saw new systems put in place for removing waste from cities so it would not make people sick.

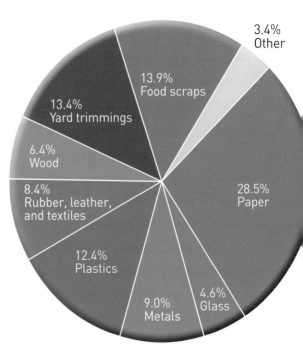

Waste

What are we throwing away?

- 3.4% Other
- 13.9% Food scraps
- 13.4% Yard trimmings
- 6.4% Wood
- 8.4% Rubber, leather, and textiles
- 12.4% Plastics
- 9.0% Metals
- 4.6% Glass
- 28.5% Paper

Source: U.S. Environmental Protection Agency

Imagine a time when garbage was left in the streets of cities.

Waste Today

Every day, each person in the United States throws away about four and a half pounds of garbage. That is about twice the amount each person threw away just 50 years ago.[1]

And that is just waste from homes. Businesses, schools, hospitals, and factories throw away even more garbage.

All together, the United States produces about 251 million tons of garbage every year. An elephant weighs one ton. So we make enough waste to equal 251 million elephants! Where would we put 251 million elephants? Or more to the point, where does all that garbage go?

[1] Source: Product Policy Institute

Where Does Waste Go?

All our trash remains on Earth in some form. More than half of our garbage ends up in **landfills**. A landfill is a site where trash is collected either in or above the ground. A

large area is dug out of the earth. Liners are placed inside the area to contain the trash. But the trash stays in the landfill. It does not break down or go away.

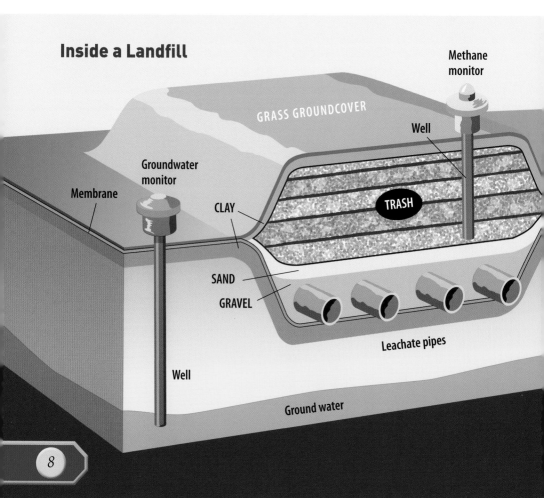

Inside a Landfill

Methane monitor

GRASS GROUNDCOVER

Well

Groundwater monitor

Membrane

CLAY

TRASH

SAND

GRAVEL

Leachate pipes

Well

Ground water

When a landfill is full, it can sometimes be put to new use. In Virginia Beach, Virginia, a park was built on top of a landfill. The park is called Mount Trashmore!

Membrane

About ten percent of our garbage goes to **incinerators** where garbage is burned. The waste does not completely go away. However, it is reduced to ash. Burning waste can put harmful chemicals into the air. Incinerators emit **carbon dioxide** (CO_2). That can be harmful to our environment.

But in some cases, the energy from burning waste can be turned into electricity. As the waste is burned, it creates steam. The steam generates energy that creates electricity. This is called **waste-to-energy**. However, this process does still create some air pollution. And ash is still left behind after the waste is burned. This ash then often ends up in landfills.

Great Pacific Garbage Patch

Imagine a mass of plastic bags, toothbrushes, toys, bottles, and Styrofoam that is as big as the state of Texas. But such a thing isn't imaginary. It's very real.

Where does plastic garbage go if it's not **recycled?** Sometimes it goes into the earth. Sometimes it goes into the water. In the Pacific Ocean, swirling currents have brought together pieces of plastic garbage. The garbage comes from Asia and North America. The whole mess is often referred to as the Great Pacific Garbage Patch.

The tangled mass of plastic in the Pacific Ocean floats just below the water's surface.

Do you think you might be interested in a career managing the safety and health of Earth's air, water and land?

PAULA ROSE

Here are just a few of the jobs you could do.

Civil Engineer   *Grant Writer*

Environmental Chemist   *Marine Biologist*

"Learn to think like a scientist. Keep exploring even when you don't know where it's taking you." That's advice from Paula Rose, marine biochemist with the Naval Research Laboratory. While studying at Stony Brook University, Paula explored medical waste in the environment. Small amounts of radioactive Iodine 131, commonly used to treat thyroid disease, are easily discharged in sewage. Her work helped trace where the chemical went. "Everything we put into our toilets or down the drain doesn't get filtered in our waste sewage process. It's usually not a public health issue, but it's important to know how it affects our water," says Paula.

When it is exposed to sun and water, plastic breaks up into tiny pieces. That is what happens to the plastic in the Great Pacific Garbage Patch. The tiny pieces of plastic float in the water. Sea birds and fish mistake the plastic for food. When they eat it, it makes them sick. Eating the plastic can also kill them.

The Great Pacific Garbage Patch was first discovered in 1997. Scientists are still trying to understand the effect it will have on Earth's health.

CHAPTER TWO

Reduce, Reduce, Reduce

Reduce, reuse, recycle. There is a reason that *reduce* is the first word in that familiar list. Reducing waste is the most important of the three. Putting less garbage into the environment is better for our land, air, and water. Garbage that breaks down in our environment releases greenhouse gases. That can lead to global warming and climate change. Reducing simply means doing your best to make less waste.

About 9,000 communities in the U.S. have curbside recycling programs.

Use Only What You Need

Waste can't harm the Earth if it doesn't exist. How can people make less waste? The simplest way to reduce waste is to remember this rule: Buy only what you need. Use everything you buy.

Sometimes we end up with things we didn't ask for. For example, gift bags or prizes often have little plastic toys that are fun in the moment, but not used much in the long run.

Cheaply made plastic items often break easily. Then they are thrown away. Plastic toys like these are sometimes given the nickname "landfill toys" because they are easily thrown out. But they are not often recyclable.

The toys might be reused in a creative way. But the greenest option is to avoid them in the first place.

DID YOU KNOW?

Each American produces about twice as much garbage as individuals in other nations around the world.

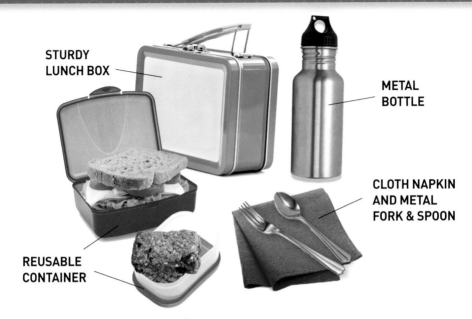

STURDY LUNCH BOX

METAL BOTTLE

CLOTH NAPKIN AND METAL FORK & SPOON

REUSABLE CONTAINER

A No-Waste Lunch

Kids can help reduce waste every day. Bringing a waste-free lunch to school helps cut down on the amount of materials to be thrown away. What does that look like?

- Use a sturdy lunch box or bag that can be reused every day.

- A metal bottle can help keep your drinks cool.

- A cloth napkin and metal fork and spoon can be washed and reused.

- Avoid prepackaged foods by making your own cookies or granola bars.

- Only bring as much food as you will eat. If you have extra food, share with a friend.

- Put food items in cloth wraps or reusable containers instead of plastic wrap or foil.

Make Waste-Free Choices

Everyone needs to eat, drink, wash, take care of themselves, and have fun. Here are some examples of choices in these areas that make less of an impact on the Earth.

Reusing paper bags and boxes is a greener choice than small plastic containers.

Try not to buy foods that have too much packaging. Choose foods with no packaging, if possible.

Try bar soap instead of bottles of body wash. They have less packaging.

Choose a big jar of applesauce (or make your own) instead of buying single-serve cups. Pack your own single-serve portion in a reusable cup.

Reduce paper waste. Think twice before printing! When printing, use both sides of a piece of paper. Keep scraps of paper to make notes and doodles. Recycle paper when it's used up.

Use rechargeable batteries. And remember, never throw old batteries in the trash. Some stores will recycle them for you.

Buy toys and gifts made of metal, cloth and wood that are sturdy and long-lasting. Or give zero-waste gifts, such as home-baked cookies.

If you only need to use something once or for a short time, borrow instead of buying. Libraries are a good green choice for books and movies.

Use a refillable water bottle instead of buying bottled water. Fill it with free tap water.

Buy reusable items. Try dishtowels instead of paper towels. Use cloth sandwich wraps instead of plastic sandwich bags.

When shopping, bring your own canvas or reusable bags instead of using plastic bags from the store.

Try to avoid plastic forks, knives, spoons, and cups. Reusable utensils and dishes are a greener choice.

FACE OFF: Ban the Bottle?

Plastic water bottles are recyclable. However, only one in five water bottles gets recycled. The rest remain on Earth, either in landfills or in our water.

"I think stores should stop selling bottled water. Tap water is free, and it's just as good. Bottled water is a waste of money and bad for the planet. People should use their own bottles and refill them for free."

The United States has some of the cleanest, safest drinking water in the world. Yet Americans spent more than 21 billion dollars on bottled water in 2011. Much of the water we buy in bottles is actually just tap water. It comes from a municipal, or city-run, source. Fossil fuel is needed to make plastic. Each year we use 17 million barrels of oil to produce plastic water bottles. Some college campuses will not sell bottled water.

"Don't ban bottled water! Water is healthier than soda. Places that have banned bottled water still sell sugary soda. Soda also comes in plastic bottles. People should be able to easily buy a healthy drink when they are thirsty."

Water is the healthiest drink. It has no sugar. It satisfies thirst. People who support selling bottled water want to have a healthy, convenient option when they buy a drink. Soda and sports drinks, which also come in plastic bottles, are less healthy. They are full of sugar and chemicals. Bottled water is also important to have on hand during water emergencies. For example, some storms, floods, or chemical leaks can make local water undrinkable.

What do you think?

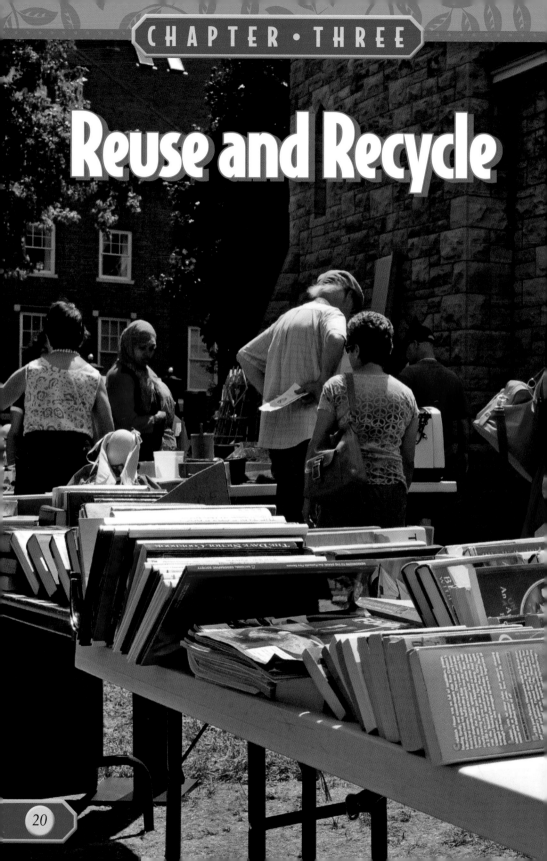

CHAPTER THREE

Reuse and Recycle

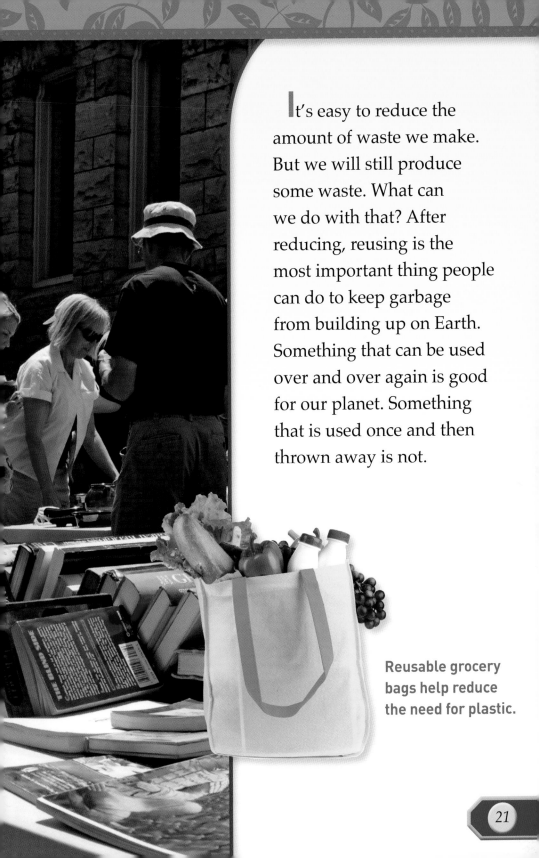

It's easy to reduce the amount of waste we make. But we will still produce some waste. What can we do with that? After reducing, reusing is the most important thing people can do to keep garbage from building up on Earth. Something that can be used over and over again is good for our planet. Something that is used once and then thrown away is not.

Reusable grocery bags help reduce the need for plastic.

Great Ways to Reuse

There are many ways to reuse. And lots of them are fun! Many books, magazines, toys, and clothes are thrown out every day. But they don't have to be. Unwanted items can be passed along to a friend or neighbor who can use them. But not everyone knows people who need these items. What then?

Some schools and community centers hold book-and-toy swaps. People can bring things they don't need anymore, and take things they would like to have – all for free.

And of course, the library is a great green choice. Anyone can borrow books and movies as often as they would like. Then they are returned so others can use them. Many libraries take donations of old books, CDs and DVDs if they are in good condition.

Some groups like Girl Scouts collect eyeglasses and other items to reuse.

Other goods can be reused and recycled as well. Old eyeglasses can be cleaned and fixed so they can be given to people who can't afford new eyeglasses. Often eye doctors will know where to donate old eyeglasses.

Electronic goods can be donated as well. Many organizations teach people how to repair things by using donated items. Then the items are given to people who cannot afford to buy new items such as lawnmowers, washers, and refrigerators.

People who update their homes can donate old cabinetry, furniture, and other household items. Organizations such as Habitat for Humanity will restore and use those items in the houses they build.

DID YOU KNOW?

It's common to end up with plastic bags. Most people reuse the plastic bags by lining wastebaskets or using them for pet waste. Now some cities have banned plastic bags.

Compost: Nature's Way of Reusing

Take a peek into a garbage can in a school cafeteria after lunchtime. It will likely be filled with food. Americans throw away about 13.2 million tons of food each year. Americans also throw away 31 million tons of grass clippings, raked leaves, and tree trimmings. Food and yard waste adds up to about 25 to 30 percent of our garbage.

Composting food and yard waste is much healthier for Earth than sending that waste to landfills. Composting breaks down natural waste by mixing it with tiny organisms such as bacteria. Composting can also be done with worms! The waste becomes a nutrient-rich material that can be added to soil to help new food and plants grow. Many cities and towns have composting programs. Some people compost at home.

Fill a home compost bin with coffee grounds, banana peels, eggshells, and other food scraps. But don't add meat and oils to your compost.

BREAK IT DOWN

What happens when waste goes into landfills? Sometimes it **biodegrades**. That means it breaks down and becomes part of the soil again. But sometimes there are chemicals in waste that are harmful to the Earth if they become part of the soil. And some items take years to break down—even thousands of years.

Try this activity to get an idea of what happens to trash in a landfill. You'll need:

- Four glass jars
- Soil
- Newspaper (small, ripped-up pieces)
- An apple core
- A small empty tin can
- A plastic spoon or plastic wrap

Fill each jar about halfway with soil. Place the newspaper in one jar, the apple core in another, the tin can in the third, and the plastic item in the fourth. Cover the garbage with soil. Moisten the soil with water. Place the jars, uncovered, in a dark place, such as a basement or closet. Every day or so, mix the soil around. Check your garbage after one month. What do you notice?

Recycling

What do a paper bag, a tin can, your favorite magazine, and an empty jar have in common? They can all be recycled!

Recycling breaks down materials so they can be used again in new products. Glass, paper, aluminum, and some types of plastic can be recycled. Recycling keeps garbage out of landfills.

Many cities and towns have recycling programs. They are also sometimes able to recycle batteries. That's good news, because batteries have chemicals that can be harmful to the Earth.

Look for this symbol. It lets people know that something can be recycled. It also shows people where to put things to be recycled. You might see this symbol on certain bins or trash containers.

Recycled glass will be melted down to make new bottles.

DID YOU KNOW?

There is no limit to the amount of times glass and aluminum can be recycled.

Reduce, reuse, recycle. Remember them in order. Try to reduce the amount of waste you throw away. Use only what you need.

Reuse as much as possible. Use things over and over again, or give them to someone else who will use them. Turn food and yard waste into compost, which is healthy for the Earth.

Whatever remains after reducing and reusing can be recycled. Find out how recycling works in your community. Encourage friends and family to recycle.

Once people know how important it is to reduce, reuse, and recycle, it becomes a part of our everyday lives. Every person's actions count toward a healthier, greener Earth.

On The Job

Name: Donny Addison

Job: Manager, Waste Reduction and Recycling, Auburn University, AL

Tell us about your job and department?

Donny Addison: We manage the recycling program for all buildings on campus. We also have recycling programs at our dining facilities. We collect recycling where food is made, so if they have a soup can or a mayonnaise tub, we recycle those.

How did you become interested in this type of work?

DA: I didn't recycle as a kid growing up in Alabama. I moved to Auburn to go to college. My freshman year in college, the place I lived in backed up to the city of Auburn's drop-off recycling center. Just out of convenience, I started recycling. I ended up changing my degree from business to environmental science. My sophomore year,

I joined an environmental awareness organization and [set] a goal of getting a recycling program started at Auburn. Over 50% of what was in our trash could be recycled. We calculated the savings we could provide to the university. The administration agreed to a pilot program. We had success there. As a senior, I worked part-time for the university to start the recycling program. When I graduated in the fall of 2005, they hired me full time. I was a recycling coordinator with no staff; it was just me. Now we have a 12-person department.

What are some ways you encourage people on campus to reduce, reuse, and recycle?

DA: We have new "hydration stations" in buildings, attached to water fountains. They're made for people's refillable water bottles.

We do competitions for the residential halls to educate students on energy and water conservation and waste reduction and recycling. We measure how much energy and water they use and how much waste they generate. Students compete to see which hall can reduce the most.

What are some other successful programs you have run on the Auburn campus?

DA: Football games are big events at Auburn. There can be more than 100,000 people on campus for a game. In an average week at Auburn, the university generates anywhere from 40 to 50 tons of trash. For one of our football games, we can generate almost the same amount in one weekend. We get in there and encourage fans to recycle. We ride around the tailgates on our Re-Cycle bike, catch people in the act of recycling, and put their photos up on the screen in the stadium. We have recycling bins at our football stadium and we work with Auburn Athletics to collect the plastic people leave behind in the stands.

What do you enjoy most about your work?

DA: Working with students. They really have a passion to create change on our campus and they come up with ideas that I haven't even thought of. When the students have a united voice, the administration is more apt to listen to them. Helping foster those ideas is a really fun part of my job.

What should kids know about waste reduction and recycling?

DA: Today's young people are going to be tasked with rethinking our systems and how we make things—making more durable goods as opposed to goods that are meant to fall apart and generate more waste. Waste reduction is something anyone can do. Doing simple things like recycling or waste reduction will help keep this planet around for future generations to enjoy as well.

Glossary

biodegrades   when items decompose or break down by bacteria or other living organisms

carbon dioxide CO_2, heavy gas formed by burning of organic matter

composting   mixing natural plant materials and waste with soil, water, and heat until everything decays to be used as a plant fertilizer

incinerator   a device or place to burn waste items at high temperature turning it to ash

landfill   a place to put waste material by burying it or covering it with soil

recycle   return waste into reusable items

waste-to-energy   a process of recovering and creating usable energy, heat, or fuel when waste is burned by an incinerator.

For More Information

Books

Tsai Parker, Wen-Chia. *Kids Can Compost.* CreateSpace, 2012.

Showers, Paul. *Where Does the Garbage Go?* HarperCollins, 1994.

Web Sites

The Story of Stuff: *See what happens to our stuff and what others are doing to reduce the use of stuff.*
http://www.storyofstuff.com/

Kids' Page: National Institute of Environmental Health and Sciences: *Information and activities to help reduce waste.*
http://kids.niehs.nih.gov/explore/reduce/index.htm

All web addresses (URLs) have been reviewed carefully by our editors. Web sites change, however, and we cannot guarantee that a site's future contents will continue to meet our high standards of quality and educational value.

Index

aluminum   26

Auburn University   28-29

batteries   26

carbon dioxide   9

climate change   13

composting   24

electricity   9

fossil fuel   19

Freecycle Network   23

garbage   5, 6, 7, 10, 13, 21, 24

Great Pacific Garbage Patch   10, 11

greenhouse gases   13

Habitat for Humanity   23

incinerators   9

landfills   8, 9, 14, 19, 25

medical waste   11

Mount Trashmore (VA)   9

New York City (NY)   6

plastic   10, 11, 14, 16, 18, 19, 26

pollution   9

recycling   26-27

reusing   16, 18, 21, 22-23, 27

Stony Brook University   11

Styrofoam   10

About the Author

Anne Flounders has lots of on-the-job experience writing for kids and teens. She has written and edited magazines, nonfiction books, teachers' guides, reader theater plays, and web content. She has also recorded narration for audio- and ebooks. Anne protects our green Earth with her husband and son in Connecticut.